CATHOLIC

AND

COLLEGE BOUND

5 Challenges and 5 Opportunities

George R. Szews

acta
PUBLICATIONS

CATHOLIC AND COLLEGE BOUND
5 Challenges and 5 Opportunities
by George R. Szews

Edited by Gregory F. Augustine Pierce
Cover and text design and typesetting by Patricia Lynch

Published by ACTA Publications, 5559 W. Howard Street,
Skokie, IL 60077-2621, (800) 397-2282, www.actapublications.com

Library of Congress Catalog number: 2008925911

ISBN: 978-0-87946-361-8

Printed in the United States of America by Imagine Print Group

Year 15 14 13 12 11 10 09

Printing 15 14 13 12 11 10 9 8 7 6 5 4 3 2

INTRODUCTION

Here are the three things I remember from my first day at college.

First, my parents and younger brother drove me to St. John's in Collegeville, Minnesota—a five-hour drive from our home in Wisconsin. When my mother saw my room in the oldest dorm on campus, she broke down and cried. "It's so small and dirty," she said through her tears.

Second, it was a hot day and my room was on the fifth floor. There was no elevator. My father and brother helped me carry up my possessions while my mother did her best to "clean up" my room with nothing but a roll of paper towels and a bar of soap.

Third, after the move in my parents were reluctant to leave, so my father suggested we get something to eat. We went to the Swan Café, where my brother had a chocolate malt and the four of us had the Sunday Fried Chicken Special. I never ate at the Swan Café again, because the food there wasn't very good.

That's it. You'd think I'd remember more about my first day, but I don't. During the next four years, of course, I learned many things that would change what I thought about the world, what I believed about God, and how I wanted to see myself as an adult. But I wasn't thinking in those broad and fundamental terms that first day. I was looking at the world in much simpler terms: I was beginning an adventure in freedom and opportunity; I was leaving home; I was becoming an adult. While book learning was the obvious reason I was going to college, the real reason had to do with growing up and moving on. Although I should have known that in those four years I would grow independent of my parents and set the course for the kind of life I would lead, what I really thought was, "I hope this is fun."

How I got to be a campus minister is a longer story than I'm going to tell here. Besides, this booklet is about you, not me. As I write this I have been working with young adult Catholics for almost twenty-five years—all at the same university campus. In those years I have watched thousands of college students come and go; young women and men who had no choice but to deal with the challenges and opportunities of "higher education." As in all things, some have dealt better with them than others. I keep in touch with former students, partly because I genuinely like them and partly because I want to see how the choices they make in college shaped their futures. I think most of them would agree with a cliché worthy of some cheesy movie but still true: "Now that I am older I understand how important the choices I made were when I was young."

From my own experience and from listening to and watching so many university students over the years, I've concluded that there are a basic set of five challenges and five opportunities every college-bound Catholic encounters, whether he or she attends a big or small, private or public school; lives at home or on campus; is in a Catholic college, a secular college or a college affiliated with another denomination. There is almost no way to skip these ten issues, unless you choose to live under a dark, moist rock for the four years (or more) you are "at school." Knowing in advance what these challenges and opportunities are may help prepare you to deal with them and engage them in a constructive and determined way. Even if, like me, you're only hoping college will be fun, you will find that the experience will change you in ways you can neither anticipate nor control. You can, however, either take part in directing that change or just let it happen to you. This booklet is an attempt to give you a heads up and maybe a little bit of advice and encouragement, but the task of responding is yours and yours alone.

Even if you're only hoping college will be fun, you will find that the experience will change you in ways you can neither anticipate nor control.

FIRST CHALLENGE

The practice and knowledge of your Catholicism will be tested.

Whether your Catholicism is important to you or you see it as only a small part of who you are, you will be asked about it and tested on it when you go to college. There are groups on almost every campus that make it their goal to engage you at least once a year on the question of your faith in Jesus Christ. If you say you don't believe in him, they will try to talk you into converting or "giving yourself over to the Lord." If you say you are Catholic, they will try to challenge the depth of your knowledge and commitment to your own faith. They may invite you, for example, to a bible study that is theoretically denominationally neutral or to a "praise and worship" meeting that they assure you is open to all Christians or even to people without any faith.

In those bible studies and prayer meetings, you may often feel you know little or nothing about your religion and may begin to question whether or not you are even really Christian. Other students, many of them friendly and filled with good will, may have memorized bible verses and use terms and concepts we don't often use in the Catholic Church. You might come to believe that you don't really "know" Jesus Christ or have not been "born again" and therefore must not have a strong or vibrant faith. This experience will present a real challenge for you. You may either decide you want to toss out your Catholicism in favor of some new denomination or form of Christianity or even some other religion.

7

Here are some things that might help you face the challenge of having your practices and knowledge of your Catholicism tested:

- Most of the students you encounter in college (unless you attend a Catholic college) don't come from what we Catholics call the "liturgical" tradition. The Mass in fact provides a disciplined proclamation of a broad selection of the scriptures over the course of a three-year cycle. Catholics who go to Mass regularly or even semi-regularly and pay even a modicum of attention to the readings and homilies know more Scripture than they think they do. We Catholics may not be able to recite "chapter and verse" of the Scriptures, but we know the stories and teachings. More importantly, we understand the underlying meaning and the literary forms of the Bible better than many of our Protestant brethren, some of whom are what we call "literalists" or "fundamentalists" in the sense that they insist that every word of the Bible must be taken literally.

- Catholics also come from what we call a "sacramental" tradition. We believe that in addition to Scripture we can encounter God through sacraments, prayer and community. So we have the seven sacraments—baptism, confirmation, Eucharist, reconciliation, matrimony, ordination and the sacrament of the sick. We also have a rich tradition of group and private prayer and devotion, including the rosary, prayers at meals, meditation and contemplation, and other "Catholic" traditions that give us comfort and courage. We also have what we call "the communion of saints," which is the community of all those living and dead who believe that Jesus Christ is, indeed, "the way, the truth, and the life," as he claimed to be. Finally, we have that marvelous invention, the Catholic parish, which is a faith community, usually in a particular geographic neighborhood but sometimes centered around a college campus or other institution, that provides a place where "all are welcome."

■ You need to know that there is no such thing as "denominationally-neutral" Christianity. Every student group that tries to recruit students on a college or university campus receives funding from some concrete denominational church. The materials used in the bible studies, the songs used in the praise and worship services, all come from somewhere. Someone paid to make them available for you. If you follow the funding you will discover which group is really behind the recruiting efforts.

■ You can be confident that while you might use different terms to describe your Christianity, Catholics are most certainly Christians. In fact, we claim to be the "original Christians," in the sense that we can trace our history all the way back to the original disciples. All the other Christian denominations can trace their history back to a time when they or their predecessors broke away from the Catholic Church. It is true that they may have had good reason to do so, since there have been many problems and abuses in the Catholic Church over the centuries and even today, but the fact is our denomination—the Roman Catholic Church—has as much claim to authenticity as any other, and in many ways we have more. Catholics are committed to ecumenical and interfaith dialogue and cooperation with all people of good will, but we need not apologize or make excuses for our Christian credentials.

- Every Catholic has been baptized and is therefore counted among those Jesus Christ claims as his own. In this sense, all Catholics have been "born again in water and the spirit" and "accepted Jesus as our Lord and master." Some of our Protestant brethren demand that we be able to name the date and place of this encounter with Jesus, but for Catholics this is an ongoing process, not a one-time decision. We encounter the presence of Jesus in the Eucharist, in the Scripture, in our parish community, and in our prayer.

- While you may decide to attend these bible studies or praise and worship services because of the invitations of college friends, you do not have to keep going if you sense that they do not respect your beliefs or religious upbringing, and you are always welcome to invite your new friends to come to Mass or a Catholic bible study with you. If they are unwilling to reciprocate, you might question their sincerity in inviting you to their events.

FIRST OPPORTUNITY

To claim your Catholicism and grow in your faith.

The chapel in which I celebrate Mass four times each weekend holds only about 400 people, so I can tell pretty much each weekend who is there and who is not. That's disconcerting to some folks, comforting to others. Several years ago I noticed a student who would show up for a couple of weeks, and then disappear for months. He would show up again perhaps for a whole semester and then be gone for the next. After he returned from one of his long absences, I stopped him after the service and invited him to go on a walk with me. (I walk every day for exercise and rarely walk alone. I find my daily walks provide an excellent opportunity for me to get to know students and the members of the parish that supports our campus ministry work. I am usually booked for my walks about two weeks in advance.)

The student agreed to go on a walk, and we set a day and time. While we were on the walk, I told the student I noticed this pattern of coming to Mass and then disappearing for long periods. He said, "You really knew when I was or wasn't coming?"

"Yup," I said. "Can you tell me what's going on with that?"

He hesitated for a second or two and then said, "I'm a little embarrassed to tell you this, Father. Those times you don't see me, I'm not sure I believe in God. I really have a hard time believing there is a God. Maybe there is just nothing out there. And beyond that, the whole story about Jesus. Maybe he was just a good man."

"There are times you do show up, though," I pointed out. "What's happening then?"

"Something has occurred that makes me think: I look up and am surprised by the beauty of a sunset, for example, or my little niece grabs my finger with her perfect hand. Suddenly, I think there has to be a God, and so I find my way back to church. My problem is I can't seem to keep believing."

The May this young man graduated, he was in a going-to-church phase. I have no idea what he's doing now, but I hope he's come to terms with the fundamental belief: that there is a God and that in Jesus Christ we have seen God's human face. That day on the walk, I was struck for the first time by how lucky I have been in my life. I have never not believed

The great opportunity of university life is that you have the time and resources to explore the dimensions of your belief.

that God is real. I have been angry at God (and the church), I have run away from God (and the church), I have betrayed God (and the church), but I have always known deep inside me—in that place where words always fail us—that God loves me. I know from the many students I speak with that this is not always the case, that students are often torn between believing and not believing. The great opportunity of university life is that you have the time and resources to explore the dimensions of your belief. You can make Catholicism your own.

Each weekend, I not only know who is there at Mass, I watch their faces, looking for clues to the joys and sorrows they bring. I listen to their voices in the responses and songs to try to understand their joys and their worries. I look at the way they sit and stand, how they shake hands during the sign of peace, how they pass the collection basket one to another, and I try to get some idea of the burdens and triumphs they are experiencing.

Here are some suggestions I have developed from all this observation about how to claim your Catholicism and grow in your faith:

- Find a place to go to Mass on or near campus and make a commitment to go on a regular basis. Most large educational institutions have some sort of campus ministry program sponsored by the Catholic Church. On many campuses they will be called the Newman Center or the Newman Parish, named after the great John Henry Newman, an English cardinal and educator. In other places they will have a saint's name. Look in the yellow pages, watch the student newspaper or bulletin boards for ads, ask around campus. If you go to a small school, there may be no formal program on campus. In this case, get yourself over to the nearest geographic parish or "shop around" until you find one you like. Then make sure you go up and introduce yourself to the priest after Mass. Tell him you are a college student and are looking for a Catholic community to hook up with. If the priest is on the ball at all, he will take your name and try to get you involved in the parish, especially with any other young adults they might have.

■ When you go to Mass, participate. Sing, pray, listen. If you have the opportunity, volunteer to be a reader or Eucharistic minister or usher, join the choir, volunteer for a soup kitchen or blood drive. This may sound funny, but when you go to Mass, be sure to put at least a dollar in the collection. I know you might be broke, and I know a dollar isn't much, but you need to do this in order to feel some ownership of your Catholicism. You're no longer living your parents' Catholicism; it has to become your Catholicism now or it most likely never will be.

■ Take advantage of educational opportunities provided by the parish or campus ministry program. When you engage a university level education, you begin to think and reason like an adult. Your Catholic education needs to keep pace with everything else you're learning or your Catholicism will be a foolish and outmoded and irrelevant belief system. Much of what you know about Catholicism and Christianity you learned as a child. You were taught as a child, using simplified formulas and explanations. There is much more to what the Church believes than you could possibly have been taught when you were younger. So, go to a lecture or class or bible study program. Join a book discussion group. Find someone to talk to about theology and Scripture.

- Get to know and spend time with other Catholic students who want to claim their faith as an adult. Opportunities are often maximized when they are shared. There will be women and men who want to explore their faith, who want to make the most of their college years in making Catholicism their own, who want a voice in shaping the church of the future.

- Get to know your parish or campus ministry staff, and let them get to know you. You are in a transition period of your life. You need mentors on your journey. These staff people will listen to your doubts and fears; they have traveled the road your on with others before you. It's important to have people who know the way ahead and are willing to help you get there.

SECOND CHALLENGE

Your moral center will be tested.

In my first year at college I wound up doing two things I never thought I would do. In the large scheme of things I can look back on it now and see they weren't awful. They didn't rise to the level of killing someone, for example, and yet one of them has probably shortened my life considerably. Before these two things happened, I thought I knew what was important to me, what was morally acceptable behavior, what I would and would not do. I thought because I'd never acted one way before I wouldn't act that way ever. I was wrong.

The first thing was smoking. Cigarettes, I mean. One cold, gray winter day during my second semester, a friend suggested I try smoking. I had never done it, I couldn't stand it, but—what the heck—college is for trying new things, right? Before the end of that semester I'd ramped up to smoking over two packs of cigarettes a day. It took me twenty-six years to shake that bad habit, begun because I was bored and on my own and there was no one to challenge what I was doing. There were plenty of people, however, who were willing to say, "Go ahead and try it; what do you have to lose?"

The other thing initially involved sleep. Both of my parents have always been early risers. I went through an adolescent phase of wanting to sleep until noon and stay up late every night, but by the time I was ready to graduate from high school I was in so many activities that getting up early was just part of what I had to do in order to fit everything in. I didn't expect a change of lifestyle because I went to college, so I signed up for an eight o'clock class my first semester. That proved to be a mistake.

To be totally honest, the first morning class I took was an incredible bore. Still, I'm not sure exactly how boring it was because I only made about one out of three of those classes per week. The result was predictable: I got a low C in the class. I think it was the first C I'd gotten since second grade. It was a shock to my system, but I got used to it. I'd been ranked eighth in my high school graduating class of 365, but I'm sure I ranked in the lower half of my college graduating class. It amazes me now how easily I transitioned from being a good student to not caring at all about my studies.

In both of these examples, my bad choices mostly hurt myself. Young people often believe that if a choice they're about to make only has consequences for themselves it's at worst morally neutral. They don't recognize that behavior is really a test of what they believe and the kind of people they want to be.

Behavior is really a test of what you believe and the kind of person you want to be.

I believe every student in his or her first semesters at college will be tested to do something they would otherwise not have imagined or considered doing. From booze, to drugs, to sex, to stealing, to cheating—you will encounter new challenges to your own personal morality. Some of these tests you will fail. Some you will meet with strength, character, determination and faith, and will come away from them all the wiser for the confrontation.

Here are some ideas for how to respond when your moral compass starts to spin:

- Expect to have your moral values tested. You were smart enough to get into college, so don't kid yourself that you can waltz through the next four years without having your sense of right or wrong tested. In fact, denying that you will face such challenges makes it all the more difficult for you to respond to them.

- Ask for advice from older adults. Balancing the do's and don'ts of certain actions is never as clear or as easy as you might think. You are entering adult life and will have to make decisions as an adult would. Simple rules are helpful to children. "Never touch the stove," makes sense when you're saying that to a two-year-old; but most of us would starve if we kept that simple rule the rest of our lives. We have to learn there are parts of the stove that are okay to touch, parts we should avoid touching, and parts we can touch if we are careful and use an oven mitt. One of the good things about college is that you will find many willing mentors among your professors and at your campus ministry center or local parish. You will also find mentors among your uncles and aunts and even your parents' friends. Most of them would be happy to help you, withholding judgment and keeping your confidence, even from your parents. They understand there are moral choices you have to make at this age and need someone to talk with about them.

■ Choose your friends carefully. Everyone knows that by the time you're eighteen the friends you choose pretty much determine the kinds of things you'll do. Few of us are strong enough to withstand constant negative peer pressure. All of us can use the support of a good friend to help us keep our resolve or our commitments. So look around, watch and listen. Then choose the friends who will help you be the kind of person you want to be. Sometimes it will be your new roommate, but other times it could be someone you meet in class, on your campus job, on a sports team, or—heaven help you—at the campus ministry center or local parish. The trick is learning to take the first step. People in college are generally open to new friends, but sometimes you have to make the first move. Invite someone to go to a campus event with you or just stop for a cup of coffee. Sometimes a good icebreaker is to ask for help with some school work. If the person responds and you hit it off, you might find you have the basis for a lifetime friendship.

■ Don't be afraid to ask for forgiveness. One of the best things about being Catholic is our belief that God is always ready to forgive. When we fail, we can make

One of the best things about being Catholic is our belief that God is always ready to forgive.

a new start. Far too many young people don't know how to ask for forgiveness. They are too ashamed, too guilty, or too unwilling to start over again. So they carry the burdens of their failure around with them and never give themselves a chance at a far more fulfilling life. You will miss out on a lot by giving up on yourself, quitting too soon just because you've failed or let someone down. Ask that person for forgiveness. You'll see that they will give it, and this really will open up new avenues in your life.

■ Build on your strengths. If you are a good listener, listen to people. If you have a sense of humor, use it. If you are passionate about something, let other people share it. You can be the kind of person others count on for leadership stability and support. Find positive pursuits and activities that expand your experiences and horizons. This will shore up your moral center by forcing you to make decisions about who you are and who you want to be. You are going to have to redefine your ideas of right and wrong in college, so turn this certain challenge into an opportunity by giving yourself as many chances to do so as you can.

SECOND OPPORTUNITY

To contribute to the common good.

Leaving the safety and security of your parents' home for the first time and entering the real world provides a genuine opportunity to contribute to the common good. Up until this point in your life, your parents did everything they could to make the world a place for you to thrive. They shuttled you back and forth between your home and your activities. They worked charity events so your athletic teams would have new uniforms or more ice time at the local hockey arena. You saw your parents working in community organizations or on local political campaigns, contributing time and money to charities, volunteering for neighborhood clean up days or delivering meals to shut-ins or sick relatives. They will continue to do these things and maybe even more now that you are gone.

But now it is your turn to begin to make this world a better place—on your own, not because your parents or your high school requires you to have "service hours" to graduate. You need to do it not for the people you might help (although they will certainly be grateful) but for your own spiritual development.

I was riding with a student one day as we passed a middle school. Suddenly, he stopped the car and got out. I hadn't noticed what he'd seen, so I watched as he went over to a group of middle school students who were standing near a Hmong grandmother and her small grandchild. It looked like some heated words were exchanged between my companion and the kids, and then the kids walked away and my friend went over and spoke with the woman. Eventually he came back into the car. "What happened?" I asked.

"Didn't you see it?" he said. "Those kids were actually throwing stones at that woman just because she was different from them! I couldn't believe it. When I went up to them they didn't even get what an evil thing it is to throw stones at helpless people. Don't you just wonder how they were raised?"

I did wonder that. But I also wondered how my young friend had been raised. He came to college ready to see the world in a new way and believing he would be given opportunities to make the world a better place. If being at college challenged his moral center at times, it also strengthened it. This young man had claimed his share of the privileges of becoming an adult in this society, but he also accepted the new responsibilities that come with it. When he dropped me off at my office I watched him drive away and believed that wherever this young man went, whatever city he lived in, whatever place he worked, whatever neighborhood he lived in, it would be a better place because he was there.

Here are some ways that you can begin to contribute to the common good while you are in college:

- Keep your eyes open. Every day there are moments like the one above where you can make a difference in the small scheme of things. Don't wait for someone else to do it (especially some older adult or authority figure). Take action yourself. You can do it, and most often you will do the right thing. And if you make a mistake, it will be easy to rectify it. Making the transition from an inner-directed, self-absorbed person to someone who notices and responds to the needs of others is one of the surest signs of maturity in a person.

■ Be proactive. This is your chance to try something new to make the world a better place. Try something new: get involved in a political campaign, work to better the environment, write for the student newspaper (even if it is only an occasional letter to the editor). This is the time in your life to try being a "good-deed entrepreneur." For example, one of the students I knew self-published a calendar featuring photographs of his university's current athletes and donated all the proceeds to cancer research. He did this project partly to hone his business skills, but he also did it to raise money for the charity. He didn't make a dime for himself, but the experience and the satisfaction he received were worth a small fortune.

Every day there are moments where you can make a difference in the small scheme of things. Don't wait for someone else to do it. Take action yourself.

- Check out your campus ministry center for possible mission or service opportunities. You could build homes for Habitat for Humanity, cook at a local homeless shelter, or sort through clothing for St. Vincent de Paul Society. Most colleges offer trips during school breaks to places that need and welcome student help. After the Katrina hurricane, for example, many college students spent a week helping the community in New Orleans and the Gulf Coast recover.

- Here's a more ambitious idea, one that you could start investigating and preparing for soon after starting your college career. You can plan on giving two years of your life immediately after college to some group like the Jesuit Volunteer Corps or the Peace Corps or some other volunteer program. Teach for America provides a host of programs you can plug into. There is a place in Chicago called Amate House where you can live and work for two years in the inner city. The University of Notre Dame offers a program where you can obtain a Masters Degree free by giving two years of service teaching in Catholic schools.

- The Roman Catholic Church has a long and good track record on social justice. Read the encyclicals and the documents of Vatican II. Your campus minister or parish priest can point you in the right direction. Take a class, join a group, do something that promotes peace and justice or works to end discrimination or abuse while you are still in college. The Vatican's Mission to the United Nations even offers a week long course every May on the social teaching of the Catholic Church just for university students. It's a great opportunity to meet people who work for the Catholic Church on social justice issues on an international basis. This is the time of your life to begin bringing life to others.

THIRD CHALLENGE

The quality and style of your life will be tested.

I grew up in a lower middle class household. My father drove big trucks all over Wisconsin. My mother stayed home with the children. We didn't have much, but I never really wanted for anything. My parents put me to work when I was young and saved most of the money I earned to pay for my college education. The fact that their two sons would go to college was an assumption on their part. Neither of them was a college graduate. In fact my father quit high school to help out on the farm and then joined the army. I was the first to go to college, my brother followed four years later. I became a priest; he's the chief operating officer of a Fortune 500 company.

Our parents taught us the basic rules of honesty, hard work, sacrificing today so that tomorrow might be better. They passed on their faith in God and the practice of the Catholic religion. They taught us how to get along with and be kind to other people. My parents were always doing something for someone else.

I never thought about how my family lived and how I was raised until I went to college and started having experiences of my own. I remember one time I was hitchhiking to Fargo, North Dakota, when I was picked up by a guy who had a handgun stuck in his pants. I suddenly realized I was a long way from where I'd started and wasn't so sure how I'd gotten there. This was one of those "Aha!" moments for me, when

I realized what was inside me and how I could, to a certain extent, choose the way I wanted to live my life.

Some of the students I meet have parents who have literally tried to kill them, who went through bitter divorces and blamed the kids, who never bought them a toothbrush because they needed the money for beer. I meet students whose siblings introduced them to booze and drugs before they were teenagers, or who beat them regularly. I meet students who spent so much time in organized sports and were so driven by their parents that they wouldn't pick up a ball or hockey stick to save their lives. I meet students who have led such lives of luxury and privilege they have never washed a dish or shoveled snow.

Everyone comes to college with a certain picture in his or her head of what life should be like. Whether that picture is explicit or not, most in-coming students assume they will continue living the same quality and style of life they had while they were living with their parents. Whether you are a child of privilege or dysfunction or both, life in college will not be the same as it was. Some students find that dizzying and distressing, others find it seductive and freeing, still others flee back home each weekend.

Here are a few methods for dealing with the inevitable changes in your lifestyle and the quality of your life once you get to college:

- The first few months of life at college are generally the most difficult. There are students who are so disoriented during those months that they assume college isn't for them, or at least *this* college isn't for them. Don't make any big decisions about staying in college or leaving your college for some other until well into your second semester. Then you can make a rational decision, not one based on the emotion caused by leaving home and being on your own for the first time. Sometimes students do make the wrong initial choices about college, and there is nothing wrong with correcting those decisions. But do so after you have given your initial choice a real chance.

■ Remember that college isn't a career. It's a temporary means to another part of your life. During this transitional period expect you will be inconvenienced and will not have the kind of life you might some day have. Expectations about the kind of food you'll get in the school cafeteria or the quality of the mattress you sleep on or how tight you and your first roommate are going to be are often disappointed. Don't worry about it. Put it all into perspective. Most of us can live through anything for five minutes—or for four years—as long as we know it is temporary.

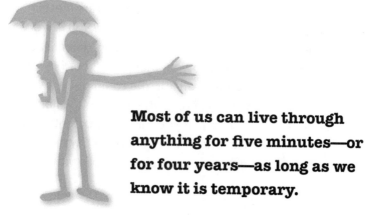

Most of us can live through anything for five minutes—or for four years—as long as we know it is temporary.

- Expect your comfort zone to be challenged. You'll be living in close proximity to people who are very different from you and were raised very differently from the way you were raised. Choose which things about the way you live that are important and which things don't matter in the short term. For example, peers who are receiving a monthly allowance while you have to earn your spending money are likely to bug you, but you'll get over it. It's not going to kill you, and it might even make your stronger, or at least more independent.

- Whether it's over money or time or number of interests, know your limits. You don't have to do everything there is to do in college, and you don't have to be the class valedictorian to be a happy, successful person. Pick and choose the things you want to do, and learn to say "no" when your newfound friends want to jump in a car and drive to Mexico for the weekend.

- While you might not live the way you did when you lived at home, you will still be able to live in *some* of the ways you used to live. Choose which are most important to you, and then figure out how you can accomplish them. If having a formal family dinner each Sunday is important to you, then figure out how to get hooked up with a family in the community. If you need time to yourself, find a little nook in the library and make it your own. If you miss your parents and siblings, call them once a week or once a day on your cell phone, or get home once a month for a visit.

■ Try new things and people. You may have come to college knowing that some things needed to change in your life. If you find yourself always hanging out with the same kind of people, or if you have grown dependent on alcohol or drugs or sex or food, or if you have questions about your faith, make some changes. Take a risk by joining a club you never thought you would. Ask someone out who is totally different from anyone you've ever dated in your life. Take a course that is about something you know nothing about.

■ If you find yourself depressed or sad or in trouble, ask for help. Every college has counseling services and support groups. Your Catholic campus ministry center or your local parish staff will be able to point you in the right direction for help. Ask for it. Take their advice. Take any challenge to the way you used to live as an opportunity to grow.

Take any challenge to the way you used to live as an opportunity to grow.

THIRD OPPORTUNITY

To explore the rich diversity of others.

Many students who go to college arrive with high school friends or knowing someone who is already enrolled there. In many cases an older sibling has gone to the college and so they are familiar with the campus and city. Few students arrive not knowing anyone or anything about their new place. (In fact, most colleges now have extensive orientation programs to prevent this situation from developing.)

For some students, pre-established connections mean they never get to know very many people or have to deal with the new environment of college. They stay in self-imposed ghettos of familiarity, which minimizes the challenges to the way things used to be in their lives. They miss entirely the tremendous opportunity going to college presents. College is a time to expand your circle of friends, experience cultural diversity, and engage in an experiential critique of your values and perspectives on life.

Most universities of any size deliberately promote international awareness. Students from other cultures come to the United States to study; students from the United States study abroad. I never took that opportunity when I was in college. I'd grown up in a small town and went to school in a small town. The truth is that I was afraid to study abroad. I didn't think I was very good at languages and really had no experience with travel. Rather than seeing study abroad as an opportunity to learn more about the world and myself, I made sure I stayed within my comfort zone. It was a mistake.

Since I didn't know anyone at my college before I arrived, I had no friend or acquaintance to room with, so I got assigned a roommate at random. He was from Hong Kong. Talk about a shock to my system! I'd never even spoken to a real Chinese person before that first day in our dorm room. Even though I was still in the middle of the Midwest, my life seemed to be spinning into something surreal. Most of the routines and patterns of ordinary life were so disrupted that I simply withdrew. I was so concerned about how uncomfortable I was feeling that I didn't step outside of my skin once to imagine how whatever I was experiencing must have been multiplied a thousand times inside my roommate. As a consequence, we never really got along. We were strangers who inhabited the same very small space for a whole year. It's possible that even if I'd felt less defensive we wouldn't have become friends. Still, a lot is determined by the first days and nights in college, and I was too busy taking care of myself to take advantage of the opportunity to grow beyond my self-absorbing fears.

Here are some ways for you to avoid the mistakes I made in not exploring the rich diversity of culture and life that college offers:

- Give your roommate a chance. Maybe you won't end up as lifelong friends, but you can learn a lot from just about everyone if try. If your roommate really doesn't work out, expand your horizons to the other people on your floor. There's got to be someone there who is different from you but still compatible. College is one of the easiest places in the world to meet someone, because everyone is basically in the same boat. You'll be surprised how responsive almost everyone is to a simple invitation to join you for lunch or a pizza or a movie or a sporting event.

- Study abroad if you get the chance. In many cases, a summer or junior year abroad will cost little extra than the plane ticket to and from the country you're studying in. Colleges work hard to make these opportunities accessible to everyone by leveling out the costs and making them about the same as staying on campus. There are often scholarships or internships or financial aid available to make it happen. You may never have another opportunity to spend a lengthy amount of time in another culture in an environment that is both safe and challenging.

- If you can't study abroad there are national exchange programs. One of the students who sang in our choir went on a national university exchange program to New Orleans the year of hurricane Katrina. He was evacuated and never really spent much time there, but living through that ordeal with several people changed his perspective on life. There are no guarantees that exploring new cultures isn't risky, but fear is a prison that makes our insides shrivel even if on the outside we appear healthy.

- Be open and curious. One of the signs a person is growing into healthy adulthood is an inquisitiveness about the people and world around him or her. One of the most disconcerting parts of the gospels is Jesus saying we will meet him in the poor and imprisoned, the thirsty and naked and hungry, the stranger. He suggests that those who are only concerned with what is familiar and comfortable in their lives will miss him completely. It may be impossible to be a disciple of Jesus and not open our eyes and ears and hearts to what is unfamiliar or fearful to us. Your curiosity during your college years will motivate you to take advantage of the opportunities to explore the incredible diversity of culture and life that is part of God's creation.

Your curiosity during your college years will motivate you to take advantage of the opportunities to explore the incredible diversity of culture and life that is part of God's creation.

FOURTH CHALLENGE:

Your assumptions about family and friends will be tested.

The first days at college for most students—if they're being honest at all—are a mix of excitement, fear, loss, loneliness, expectation and surprise. I may have experienced more emotions and learned more about myself in my first month of college than I did the rest of the time I spent at St. John's. One of the biggest changes I had to deal with was my relationship with my family and my friends back home.

During those first weeks I was totally surprised and ambushed by a shyness I'd never experienced in high school. I'd been class president and president of the student body. I'd played sports and been in a play. I'd been co-editor of the yearbook. I was a doer and a talker. But at college I didn't know a soul. Worse, I didn't know how to meet anyone. Unlike many people who choose the college they want to attend based on where their friends are going, I'd gone to St. John's because I didn't know anyone there. That sounded exciting when I was filling out the application papers, but it wasn't so great the first morning I went to the cafeteria for breakfast and sat alone eating soggy cornflakes. I kept thinking this was such a mistake, perhaps the biggest mistake I'd made in my life.

I missed my family, certainly. I guess you would say I was homesick, but not in the sense that I wanted to return home. It was more that I realized I wasn't a kid anymore and never would be, and that my relationships with my parents,

We realize we need to make new friends, which inevitably means we adjust how we interact with the friends we already have.

my brother, and my other relatives had changed forever, and I hadn't even seen it coming.

Even more I missed my friends. I guess we had all thought we'd be friends for life, and now we didn't even see one another. We had been through a lot together. We knew what we each thought about things. We had one another's back. While I didn't have a serious girlfriend that I had left behind, I certainly had girls that I knew and with whom it was easy to talk. In college, I seemed to be tongue-tied and awkward.

I think most people who move away from home for the first time experience similar mixed emotions. I also believe that for most people those feelings don't linger. They are intense and offer us insights into what we truly value, but then we adapt to the new people and surroundings and these feelings subside. We edge our way toward the boundaries of our comfort zone and realize we need to make new friends, which inevitably means we adjust how we interact with the friends we already have.

Here are some tips for redefining your existing relationships with family and friends:

- Realize that when you leave home to go to college you are not saying "goodbye" to your family and friends as much as you are saying, "Our relationship is going to change." There is no need to be explicit about this. It will happen naturally. Just don't be surprised when it does.

- Get yourself a calendar and write all of the important birthdays and anniversaries of your family and friends. Look at the calendar each week and send out a card or a letter, either by mail or e-mail, or make a phone call to let the person know you are thinking about him or her. (It will also remind you to think of them, which will make you feel better as well.) Computers and the Internet now have all kinds of programs that will remind you of these dates and provide fun greetings you can send at virtually no cost.

- Stay in touch with your friends from high school while you or they are away at college, and visit with them whenever you or they return home for a visit.

But don't expect the level of your relationship to remain where it was in high school. You are moving on, and so are they.

- If your family or friends react that you are "changing" or "losing touch" with them, don't be defensive. Tell them that you still care about them and are interested in what they are doing. But be willing to talk about the new interests and activities in your life, and ask them to talk about theirs.

- Long distance dating relationships are a struggle to maintain. The inability to spend time with your boyfriend or girlfriend every day will change it, no matter how often you call or text message each other. The relationship you bring with you to college, which was based on the amount of time you spent together in high school, can no longer be what it once was. Your relationship will survive only if you have some things in common that are deeper. A history together will never completely compensate for a present and future together.

FOURTH OPPORTUNITY

To establish an adult relationship with yourself and others.

Two things converge to change the way you will relate to people when you go to college. First, you move into a new environment that demands you change and adapt. Second, you are transitioning to a new stage in your life in which you are capable of deeper and more authentic emotional commitments. These provide you with an incredible opportunity to engage in loving behaviors at their deepest and best levels.

I enjoy hearing from former students. Late one summer a recent graduate sent me an email telling me his Teach for America training had been completed. He said those weeks of training had been the toughest of his life. He had been given a class of students for a summer catch-up program. They were totally uninterested in anything he was supposed to teach them. He wrote in part:

The last week was especially difficult. Everyone was sick of learning and no one wanted to be there. The kids were loud, disrespectful and overall ridiculous, I decided to change my lesson from thesis sentences to respect. I defined three forms of respect; respect yourself, respect others, respect your environment. I asked all the students to think of examples of each.

Already I could see that this was going to become a chance for some of the students to trash others or get someone else in trouble. That was when I began to talk about myself. I told the students about my middle school days. About all the detentions I served and the bad grades I had received. I told them about the high school progress report where I received a D- and an F. I told them about the time when I got in trouble with the cops. Suddenly the mood in the class changed. For the first time all summer, all eyes were locked on me. I asked if anybody else wanted to share and a myriad of hands shot up. The ensuing discussion was one of the most interesting of my entire life. Each student had his or her own story to tell. One spoke about his friends beating up homeless men in the area for no other reason than that they could. Another spoke about getting arrested for trying to steal someone else's hubcaps...when he was ten. They talked about middle school life, bullying and bad influences. For the first time all summer there was no talking while others were talking or laughing at the quiet kids. There was simply respect.

One of the most incredible opportunities going away to college affords students is the chance to transform your personal relationship to self.

What had always intrigued me about this former student were the signs of a maturity I'd seen developing but hadn't blossomed yet. During his college years he had spoken to me about many of the things he summarized to those students that day. He talked about being bullied because he was small; about how he was shy around girls and so never really dated in high school; about being uncoordinated at athletics and trying to prove his "coolness" by getting into trouble. During college those impediments, which seem so crippling when he was in middle and high school, came to be put into their proper perspective. What had really happened that summer is that this young man had grown up. He began to have an adult relationship *with himself*, and by so doing he could have one with the students in his class. He became the adult he needed to be in order to help them.

One of the most incredible opportunities going away to college affords students is the chance to transform your personal relationship to self. You can break the patterns of how you perceive yourself. You can step back from yourself and see the child who was once overweight or shy or almost anything doesn't have to be that way any more.

When I first began writing this introduction to college life some of the people to whom I showed this outline thought this section would be about sex. Most fundamentally it is not, but it is as well. I am firmly convicted that it is only as we grow into adulthood and mature in our relationship with ourselves that we become capable of entering into adult relationships with others, including romantic relationships.

Here are some helps to grow in an adult relationship with yourself and others:

- Forgiveness is an essential part of maturing as an adult. At this point in your life you can go ahead and forgive the school bullies, the incompetent or mean-spirited teachers, the girlfriend or boyfriend who dumped you, the unjust manager at the place you worked weekends. Adults learn how to put the past behind them and look forward to the future.

- It's possible that in college or shortly afterwards you will meet the one person with whom you will spend the rest of your life. You won't do this if you are just in the hunt for sex or for someone to take the place of your parents. What you need is not to seek an unlimited supply of potential spouses to date but to take advantage of the limited window you have to become an adult. The rest will follow naturally.

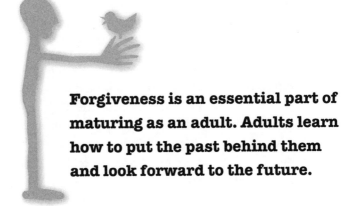

Forgiveness is an essential part of maturing as an adult. Adults learn how to put the past behind them and look forward to the future.

- One of the great temptations is to come to college believing there is little to learn–either about the world or about relationships. On the other hand, if you believe you are not yet a mature human being but want to work to become one, you will find ways to make that happen while you are at school.

- I always tell incoming students I'm not worried about the eighteen-year-old who goes to house parties and drinks too much. I worry about the senior who goes to house parties and drinks too much. College is the time to develop an adult relationship with controlled substances–from alcohol to tobacco to drugs. Until you do, you cannot function in the adult world.

- You may not keep any of your high school friends, but in college you can make a friend or two that could last a life time. During these four or five years your personality and character will stabilize. You will become the person you're supposed to be. That makes it more possible for you to make lasting friendships, including committing yourself to intimate relationships.

- When you become involved at your Catholic campus ministry center or local parish, take the opportunity to become an adult member of the church. Don't demand that the liturgies or education programs or service opportunities be tailored to young adults. Get involved with adults or all ages in real activities for adults. Make a contribution when they pass the basket, even if you can only afford a buck.

FIFTH CHALLENGE

There will be surprises.

I sat in my office with three weeping college women. They represented a group of friends who wanted an on-campus memorial service for a fellow classmate who had committed suicide. None of the three went to church, only one had been raised Catholic. They had come to see me in much the same way they might go to a caterer. They were ordering a service.

They told me what they wanted the service to look like. One insisted I never mention God because the deceased didn't believe in God. Another told me that my main job was to assure everyone that their friend was in heaven. And, they all agreed they didn't want any "churchy" music or any reading from the Bible.

What could I say? What would you have said to them?

These three women had come up against something they hadn't expected in college. They, like all of us who start out young and strong, believed that they were invincible. Nothing really bad was ever going to happen to them, and the death—much less the suicide—of one of their friends wasn't even on their radar screen.

When you go off to college, there will be surprises: things you never expected to encounter, never thought you would have to deal with, cannot control or avoid, and for which you cannot prepare. You may suddenly discover deep-seated bigotry in a person who was becoming a friend.

Someone may grow dependent on you in a very unhealthy way. You may struggle with or even fail a course for the first time in your life. You might be hauled into court because you made a stupid mistake driving or were at the wrong place at the wrong time. Your mother may discover she has breast cancer. Your father may leave her for another woman.

There are also more positive surprises in college: things you never expected that delight, intrigue or astound you. You may meet someone your first year whom you intensely dislike, and then the next year you have to do a group project together and the person becomes a close friend or even a romantic interest. In middle school you hated your teachers, but in college you may decide to become one. You may discover you have a vocation: to the priesthood or religious life, as a lawyer or a writer or a politician, as a spouse and parent. You may discover that your Catholic faith has become more real to you than he had ever been when you were growing up.

Here are some methods for dealing with surprises, both good and bad:

- When you are surprised by tragedy, share your grief. Those three young women who came to me about their friends' death had the right instinct. They knew they needed to share their sadness with others; they were just going about it in the wrong way. Go to your friends, call your parents, contact the people in campus ministry or student counseling. Listen to them; they have been through this before. They will help you deal with it. A grief ignored can only fester until it becomes a cancer that eats away at you.

■ When you are surprised by joy, share that as well. There is nothing that a college campus needs more than the enthusiasm and passion of its students. As you discover new things and new people, share that with others. If you are energized by a particular class, teacher or subject, let you friends and family know. Much like sorrow, joy that is bottled up inside you has nowhere to go.

■ When you are surprised by adversity, ask for help. If you are having trouble with your schoolwork, if you are broke and can't find a part-time job, if you are feeling depressed or anxious or scared, don't be afraid to say, "Can you help me?" You'll be surprised what magic words those are, especially on a college campus, where almost *everybody*—from the teachers to the administrators to the staff to the student body—*views their role* as helping students with their problems. You will be making their day if you ask for assistance!

■ When you are surprised by infatuation, take a deep breath and stand back for a moment. Infatuation is a powerful emotion, and it is especially strong among young adults, who are just learning what and whom they love. So, you can be infatuated by a particular kind of music, or by a teacher or a friend, or by a counselor or advisor, or by another man or woman. It's OK. Enjoy it. But do put your emotional brakes on, at least a little. Infatuation, by definition, does not last. It must turn into love for that, and love takes longer to develop because it is based on experience over a period of time. So, enjoy the ride, but make sure you get off the roller coaster long enough to get your feet planted firmly back on the ground.

■ When you are surprised by your own vulnerability, pray for strength and humility. This is a big one because most college students do not like to admit that they are vulnerable. After all, you are on your own now, trying to act like an adult. Doesn't any show of vulnerability prove that you are still a kid? Actually, no. Ask any adult and they will tell you how vulnerable they feel. It is part of the human condition, and admitting to one's vulnerability is not a sign of immaturity: it is a sign of your maturity. That's why praying for strength and humility is so powerful. You are basically saying, "You are God, and I am not." This is a very important thing for us to recognize at all times.

■ When you are surprised by injustice, work to make the world a better place. The only alternative, really, is cynicism: "The world is a bad place and there's nothing I can do about it." This is no attitude for a young person. (It's no attitude for a middle-aged or older person, either.) One of the things about being a Christian is that we have a never-ending supply of optimism that God is changing the world for the better through our actions. Jesus called this "building the kingdom of God…on earth as it is in heaven." So, when you see an injustice, do something about it, even if you're not sure what to do and even if you don't succeed. God will take care of the rest.

- When you are surprised by goodness, thank God. If you let yourself, you will be surprised by goodness all the time. There is the goodness of creation itself, the goodness of your family and friends, the goodness of the people at your college, the goodness of people with whom you work and go to school. What is easy is to ignore all this goodness and focus on the bad things. That is why it is important to thank God on a regular basis. In fact, the Catholic Mass is also called the Eucharist, which means "thanksgiving." So if you go to Mass, you can't help but give thanks for all you have.

When you are surprised by goodness, thank God. If you let yourself, you will be surprised by goodness all the time.

FIFTH OPPORTUNITY

To respond to problems and crises with character, thoughtfulness and faith.

One of my friends is an assistant dean of students. Some years back she stopped me as I was walking along. "You wouldn't believe what just happened to me," she said.

"I can't imagine," I said.

"I just got a call from a parent," she said.

"Oh, I guess I could have imagined that," I laughed.

"No, you couldn't imagine why that parent called me. This is the first time it's ever happened. Her daughter had awakened with a sore throat this morning and wouldn't be able to take a quiz. The parent asked me to go over to her daughter's class and explain to the professor that her daughter had a sore throat. Since when did twenty-year-old women have their parents run interference for them with professors? How will this student ever grow up?"

Over the years as a campus minister, I've grown convinced that fewer and fewer students have learned how to solve problems on their own. When the students were in high school, their parents never forced them to deal with a mean teacher or exclusionary coach. Wanting to give their children a good life, many parents did too much for their children, including helping them inordinately to get into college.

What happens, of course, is pretty predictable. When students finally get on their own in college, what should be problems to solve become crises of such immense proportions that students are immobilized, without a clue how to respond in an adult manner.

My first weekend in this campus ministry job was a hot one. There was no air conditioning at that time anywhere in our facility. I was working in my office after Saturday evening Mass, dressed only in a tee-shirt and some shorts. The sweat was rolling off of me. I heard a faint knock at my open door. Then there was a very timid voice, "Can I come in?"

A student entered, and he looked awful. "Wow," I said, "You look awful."

"I feel awful," he said through a trembling voice. Then he began to cry.

He sat down, eventually regained his composure, and told me a sad tale. He had been going with a girl for two years. He was sure she was "the one." Four days earlier she had dumped him. It came out of the blue. He hadn't been able to eat, sleep, concentrate or do anything since that conversation. She wouldn't talk to him. His parents told him he needed to go talk to someone, and the campus ministry center seemed to be the only place other than the bars open on a Saturday night. He figured the church was a better choice than the bars, and that's why he was there.

I told him there was bad news and there was good news. The good news was that he would live. That he would love again. That he would meet someone some day and they would fall in love and probably have beautiful children. The bad news was that tonight he wouldn't believe me. Tonight

Even though there is a difference between a problem and a crisis, you can deal with both of them in responsible and effective ways.

he would still feel like his world had ended. The bad news was that there was no way for him to avoid his suffering. It came with loving. But, I reassured him, you will live. And I told him that next weekend, when he was at Mass (see how sneaky I was even back then?) I would remind him that he was still alive.

The young man had one more year left at the university. During that year he came to Mass every Saturday evening and sat in exactly the same place at the end of an aisle. As I walked past him in the opening procession each week, I'd lean over and say, "I see you're still alive," and he'd always smile back.

This student did rise to the occasion. Certainly, it was painful for him to lose his first love, and he did suffer, but he did survive. He somehow learned to respond to his crisis with character, thoughtfulness and faith.

Nearly twenty-two years since I first met him, that same man came back to church at the campus one Saturday evening. I was standing at the door greeting people on the way out, and he shook my hand and said, "Do you remember me?"

It took me a second, but then I remembered him and said, "Sure I do, and I notice that you're still alive."

He smiled broadly and said, "Not only am I alive, but I have brought my three children for you to meet. They are beautiful, aren't they?"

"Yes, they are," I said, reaching my hand out to each of the kids.

"Thank you," he then said to me. "I needed to come back and tell you that your words have come back to me over and over again when I've encountered trouble or problems. 'You will survive,' you told me, and I've come to believe that. Every time I look at my children I know how important it was for me to pick myself up that night and go on. Thank you."

As a college student, you will encounter problems. It comes with the territory. And you will also have a few crises, although I hope not too many. Even though there is a difference between a problem and a crisis, you can deal with both of them in responsible and effective ways. In some cases you may need to ask for help or advice, but you should be able to resolve most situations you encounter. One thing that I can promise is that you will survive. These situations are really incredible opportunities to learn how strong and competent you are as a human being, how much your faith supports you in difficult times, and how grateful you are for the life and gifts you have been given.

Here are some ideas for dealing with problems and crises with character, thoughtfulness and faith:

- When you encounter a minor problem, try to resolve it on your own. If the problem includes dealing with another person, then politeness, clarity, and a genuine desire to have the situation resolved in a timely manner goes a long way. A friend of mine always says, "Think and do. It's what we learned in fourth grade, and it usually works." Don't go off half-cocked. Take a deep breath, stand back, and try to see the situation from the other person's point of view. And be willing to compromise. You don't have to have everything your own way. In fact, I can pretty much promise that you won't, but finding a solution and putting a problem behind you is often better than "winning" an argument. Half a loaf is seriously better than no loaf at all.

- If you've tried to solve a problem but don't seem to be getting anywhere, ask for advice. Explain the situation in as clear and unemotional language as possible, so the person you've asked for insight can both understand and counsel you correctly. Don't try to convince the person you are "right" and get him or her on your side. Instead, ask for help in coming up with a solution.

- A second opinion never hurts either. Remember, you're only asking for advice. You are the one who has to decide exactly what to do, when to do it, and how to do it. Even more importantly, *you* have to do it. Don't ask someone (especially your parents or your academic advisors) to do it for you. Be a man or a woman and resolve the problem yourself. (In fact, if your parents offer to do it for you, politely tell them that you can handle it and then do so. They will be delighted and amazed.)

■ If you've tried everything you and your advisors can think of, then ask for help from someone in authority. But even then, don't expect them to fix things for you. There may need to be a mediation or intervention or arbitration or even (in worst cases) a legal or quasi-legal procedure to resolve something, but don't go there first and don't think that it removes your obligation to take adult responsibility and action.

■ If your world truly seems to be falling apart, what we call a "crisis," then you are going to need more help. But you can still handle the situation in an adult manner. First of all, true crises don't occur every day or week or month. In fact, if you are lucky, you'll only have one or two during your entire college career. So the first thing is to recognize that every problem is not a crisis. If you (or someone else) is not going to die or be seriously hurt, then it is probably not a crisis. So deal with it accordingly.

■ On the other hand, if it is a true crisis, it is important that you recognize it as such. One of the signs is that you get very emotionally upset and cannot do your work. Another is when your friends start asking what is wrong or even suggest that you seek counseling of some sort. Listen to these warnings and then do something about it.

- If you need time off from college or your job or your sports team to deal with a crisis, take it. But do so responsibly by notifying your teachers or employer or coach what you are doing and why. They will understand and help you navigate the system.

- If your world truly seems to be falling apart and you don't seem to be able to pick up the pieces, please seek professional help. Most colleges have competent counseling services that will help you deal with death; trauma; abuse; alcohol, drug and food addictions; and a host of other things. Ask your friends to go with you to get help. They will be glad that they can do something for you.

- In the absolute worst possible case, where you feel that taking your own life is the only answer, reach out to someone—anyone—and tell him or her what you are thinking. It could be a friend, a minister, a member of your family, a teacher or administrator, even a doctor or police officer. Any of these people will help you. Remember: the only way you will *not* survive your crisis is if you do not stay alive to do so.

- Be courageous. Be a hero. Heroes are people who experience fear and difficulty but still do the right thing. Fools don't experience fear. Heroes know there is plenty of stuff out there that is scary, but they still find the courage to go on. You can too. Do the right thing in difficult circumstances because you love someone and someone loves you. If you don't think anyone loves you, you are wrong. God loves you, even if no one else does.

■ Finally, pray. Pray always, as St. Paul suggested. I am not saying this because I am a priest but because I have prayed many times myself. In difficult situations, prayer reminds us that we are not alone and that our resources are always greater than what we can see at any given moment. You must respond yourself to your problems and crises, all prayer can do is help. And it will.

Do the right thing in difficult circumstances because you love someone and someone loves you. If you don't think anyone loves you, you are wrong. God loves you, even if no one else does.

Prayer of the Hurried Student

Dear God,
I am on the run again,
between classes and papers and work,
and—if I'm honest—some good times.
But I do not want to run from you
or believe you are ever far from me.

Help me to be grateful today
for everything I received yesterday.
And, tomorrow, show me the path
that will lead me to do
what I know to be right and true and good.

Watch over those whom I love
and bring us all
into the Kingdom that your Son preached
would come
"on Earth as it is in Heaven."

Amen.

© George Szews

A Prayer to the Holy Spirit

Come, Holy Spirit.

Guide my days and deeds.
Give me healing in my soul,
love in my life,
and strength for my task on earth.

When I am discouraged,
grant me hope.
When I am sad,
show me the way ahead.
And when I want to deviate from the way of Jesus,
bring me back gently, surely, wholly.

On the last day,
when my life is spent,
may you be my last breath in this world
and my first in the next. Amen

© George Szews

A Prayer to Jesus

Christ, I turn to you now,
searching for you in the light of this day,
the promise of morning,
the heat of noon,
the shade of evening.

Do not let me miss you,
or mistake you for some worry or burden.
Do not let me pass you by,
as an inconvenience or obstacle.
Do not let me lose you,
in the rush to rest or the delay of boredom.

When I am weary, renew my strength.
When I am lost, find me.
When I would choose some other companion,
some other joy, some other cause,
love me as only you can.

In your goodness, give me a sense of purpose
and meaning in my daily life.
Show me here and there along the way
my bright and beckoning end,
the horizon that draws me beyond
the distractions of this world
and my own weakness
to your promise of heaven,
which is not the end of my life,
but only the beginning. Amen.

© George Szews

The Sign of the Cross

In the name of the Father, and of the Son,
and of the Holy Spirit. Amen.

The Lord's Prayer

Our Father, who art in heaven
     hallowed be thy name;
thy kingdom come, thy will be done,
     on earth as it is in heaven.

Give us this day our daily bread;
     and forgive us our trespasses,
as we forgive those who trespass against us;
     and lead us not into temptation,
     but deliver us from evil. Amen.

The Prayer of Praise

Glory be to the Father,
     and to the Son,
     and to the Holy Spirit.
As it was in the beginning,
     is now and ever shall be,
     world without end. Amen.

The Morning Offering

O Jesus, through the Immaculate Heart of Mary, I offer you
all my prayers, works, joys, and sufferings of this day, for all
the intentions of your Sacred Heart, in union with the holy
sacrifice of the Mass throughout the world, in reparation for
my sins, for the intentions of all our associates, and for the
general intention recommended this month. Amen.

Grace Before Meals

Bless us, O Lord, and these thy gifts,
     which we are about to receive,
from thy bounty,
     through Christ, Our Lord. Amen.

Prayer for Those Who Have Died

May the souls of the faithful departed,
     through the mercy of God, rest in peace. Amen.

Eternal rest grant unto them, O Lord,
     and let perpetual light shine upon them. Amen.

May they rest in peace. Amen.

The Act of Contrition

O my God, I am heartily sorry for having offended you, and I detest all my sins, because of your just punishments, but most of all because they offend you, my God, who are all good and deserving of all my love. I firmly resolve, with the help of your grace, to sin no more and to avoid the near occasion of sin. Amen.

Come, Holy Spirit

V. Come, Holy Spirit,
   fill the hearts of your faithful.
R. And kindle in them the fire of your love.

V. Send forth your Spirit,
   and they shall be created.
R. And you shall renew the face of the earth.

Let us pray.
Lord, by the light of the Holy Spirit,
you have taught the hearts of your faithful.
In the same Spirit, help us to choose what is right,
and always rejoice in your consolation.
We ask this through Christ, our Lord. Amen.

The Hail Mary

Hail Mary, full of grace; the Lord is with thee;
blessed are thou amongst women,
and blessed is the fruit of thy womb, Jesus.

Holy Mary, mother of God, pray for us sinners,
now and at the hour of our death. Amen.

Hail, Holy Queen

Hail, Holy Queen, Mother of Mercy, our life,
our sweetness and our hope.
To thee do we cry, poor banished children of Eve,
to thee do we send up our sighs,
mourning and weeping in this vale of tears.

Turn, then, most gracious advocate.
thine eyes of mercy toward us;
and after this our exile,
show unto us the blessed fruit of thy womb, Jesus.

O clement, O loving, O sweet Virgin Mary.

Pray for us, O holy Mother of God,
that we may be made worthy
    of the promises of Christ.

The Memorare

Remember, O most gracious Virgin Mary,
that never was it known,
that anyone who fled to your protection,
implored your help, or sought your intercession,
was left unaided.

Inspired by this confidence, I fly to you,
O Virgin of Virgins, my Mother.
To you do I come, before you I stand,
    sinful and sorrowful.

O Mother of the Word Incarnate,
    despise not my petitions,
but in your mercy hear and answer me. Amen.